ULTIMATE MACHINES

Trucks

Rob Colson

WAYLAND

Published in paperback in 2014 by Wayland
Copyright © Wayland 2014

Wayland
338 Euston Road
London NW1 3BH

Wayland Australia
Level 17/207 Kent Street
Sydney NSW 2000

Senior editor: Julia Adams
Produced by Tall Tree Ltd
Editor, Tall Tree: Jon Richards
Designer: Ed Simkins

British Library Cataloguing in Publication Data

Trucks. -- (Ultimate machines)
 1. Trucks--Juvenile literature.
 I. Series
 629.2'24-dc23

 ISBN: 978 0 7502 8139 3

Printed in China

10 9 8 7 6 5 4 3 2 1

Wayland is a division of Hachette Children's
Books, an Hachette UK company.
www.hachette.co.uk

Picture credits
cover top Louise Roach/Dreamstime.com,
cover bl Mashe/Dreamstime.com, cover bc ETF
European Truck Factory GmbH, 1 Yocamon/
Dreamstime.com, 2 Ritu Jethani/Dreamstime.
com, 4-5 Sportster883/Dreamstime.com, 5t yasar
bayar/Dreamstime.com, 5b Cflorinc/Dreamstime.
com, 6 Louise Roach/Dreamstime.com,
7t ollirg/Shutterstock.com, 7b Sofiene Issaoui/
Dreamstime.com, 8l Baloncici/Dreamstime.com,
8–9 Yocamon/Dreamstime.com, 9t Christian
Lagereek. Fahraeus/Dreamstime.com, 10 Ritu
Jethani/Dreamstime.com, 11t GNU, 11b Ken
Cole/Dreamstime.com, 12 Andre van Huizen/
Alamy, 13t José Marafona/Dreamstime.com,
13b Christian Delbert/Dreamstime.com,
14b Raimond Spekking/GNU, 14–15 Robert
Pernell/Dreamstime.com, 15t Larry Jordan/
Dreamstime.com, 16–17 Walter Arce/
Dreamstime.com, 17t Jim Parkin/Dreamstime.
com, 17br Brendan Howard/shutterstock,
18l Javier Sánchez/Shutterstock.com 19 ETF
European Truck Factory GmbH, 20 Gorgios/
Dreamstime.com, 21t Wikibofh/GNU, 21b Barry
Salmons/Shutterstock.com, 24 Louise Roach/
Dreamstime.com

Contents

Go trucking

Trucks are large road vehicles designed to carry heavy loads. They come in many different shapes and sizes, from small pickup trucks to enormous road trains.

We rely on trucks to deliver goods to the shops, or sometimes to our doors. Every year, trucks in the US cover a total of more than 500 billion kilometres. That is the distance from Earth to Jupiter!

In the United States, 70 percent of all goods are transported by truck.

Articulated trucks

Most large trucks have two parts to them. They are known as articulated trucks. The tractor unit at the front contains the engine and the cab, where the driver sits. Attached to the back of the tractor unit is a trailer, which holds the cargo.

Amazing design

A concrete mixer is a special kind of truck used on building sites. Instead of a trailer, it pulls a huge rotating cylinder called a drum. Inside the drum, water is mixed with cement, gravel and sand to make concrete. The concrete is mixed while the truck is driving to the building site, so that it is ready for use as soon as the truck arrives.

Freshly mixed concrete pours out of the drum of a concrete mixer. The concrete is guided into place along a narrow chute.

Peterbilt

The biggest truck manufacturer in the United States is the Peterbilt company. It makes large trucks that pull heavy loads over long distances.

The engine in most Peterbilt trucks is in front of the cab. This gives the tractor unit a long-nose shape that makes it instantly recognisable.

A long truck journey may last several days. Behind the cab in this Peterbilt there is a sleeping area with a bed for the driver to rest during long trips.

TECHNICAL DATA

Peterbilt 389 (tractor unit)

YEARS OF PRODUCTION
2006–present
ENGINE SIZE **15 litres**
NUMBER OF CYLINDERS **6**
TRANSMISSION **Manual/automatic**
GEARBOX **18-speed**
NUMBER OF WHEELS **10**
FRONT AXLE WEIGHT
10,000 kg
FUEL CAPACITY
568 litres

Amazing design

The huge grill at the front of the Peterbilt is its radiator. A truck's engine produces a lot of heat and can quickly get too hot. The radiator helps to keep the engine cool. Water is pumped through spaces around the engine called ducts. The heat from the engine is transferred to the water. The water is then passed through the radiator, where it cools down again ready to be pumped back into the ducts.

As the truck moves forwards, air flows over the radiator, cooling the water inside it.

exhaust pipe

Pipes and cans

On each side of a Peterbilt, there is a long pipe and a large metal can. The pipes are the truck's exhaust pipes, which carry away waste gases from the engine. The cans are air filters. They suck in air and remove any dirt from it. The engine needs this clean air to burn its fuel. Any dirt in the air would clog up the engine and stop it from working.

air filter

Cabover trucks

A cabover truck is a truck with the engine underneath the driver's cab. It has a shorter tractor unit than the Peterbilt truck (pages 6–7).

Cabover trucks are popular in parts of the world, such as Europe, where there are rules that limit the length of a truck. The shorter tractor unit allows them to pull a longer trailer.

Amazing design

In a cabover truck, the whole of the cab tips forwards to allow a mechanic to work on the engine. Truck engines are very big and heavy. The engine of a large truck may weigh more than 1 tonne – heavier than some cars.

Spoiler

A truck needs to be as aerodynamic as possible. This means that it needs to move through the air as easily as possible. When a truck is pulling a tall load, a curved spoiler is fitted to the roof of the cab to deflect the air around it.

TECHNICAL DATA

Volvo FM (tractor unit)

YEARS OF PRODUCTION **2008–present**

ENGINE SIZE **12.8 litres**

NUMBER OF CYLINDERS **6**

TRANSMISSION **Manual**

GEARBOX **14-speed**

NUMBER OF WHEELS **6**

FRONT AXLE WEIGHT **9,000 kg**

FUEL CAPACITY **Up to 870 litres**

With the engine right underneath his feet, the driver of this Volvo FM truck gets a very good view without a nose in front of the cab.

Pickup trucks

A pickup truck is a small truck with an open-top area at the back. This area is called the cargo bed, and is used to carry the truck's load.

Pickup trucks are the same size as a large car, so they can reach places bigger trucks cannot go.

The Dodge Ram is a large pickup truck made by the American company Chrysler. This model has four doors and room inside for four people to sit. Smaller pickup trucks just have two doors and two seats.

TECHNICAL DATA

Dodge Ram 1500

YEARS OF PRODUCTION **2009–present**

ENGINE SIZE **3.7 litres**

NUMBER OF CYLINDERS **6**

TRANSMISSION **Automatic**

GEARBOX **4-speed**

NUMBER OF WHEELS **4**

WEIGHT **2,270 kg**

FUEL CAPACITY **197 litres**

Two steel bars called rails run the length of the chassis.

The rails are connected by crossmembers.

Amazing design

A heavy truck needs to be very strong to support its weight. Most of its strength is provided by a steel frame called a chassis. The chassis of a pickup truck stretches the whole length of the truck, supporting the weight of the truck and its cargo. All the other parts of the truck are attached to the chassis.

Tailgate

At the back of a pickup truck is a door called a tailgate. The tailgate is hinged at the bottom. It can be lowered to allow cargo to be loaded onto the truck, or to make room for long cargo.

This truck's tailgate has been lowered to fit on more firewood. A chain on either side of the tailgate supports the weight of the load.

Dumper trucks

A dumper truck is a type of truck used to transport loose material, such as sand or gravel.

The loose material is loaded into the hopper at the back of the truck. When the dumper truck reaches its destination, it empties the load by tipping up the front of the hopper. This makes the load slide out at the back.

Amazing design

Haul trucks are special dumper trucks used in quarries to carry away the broken-up stone. Haul trucks are giant vehicles and their wheels may be several metres high. The cab is above the wheels, and the driver has to climb a ladder to reach it. The largest haul truck in the world, the Liebherr T282B, can carry up to 400 tonnes of stone at a time.

Giant haul trucks such as the Liebherr T282B are specially designed to be used off-road. They are far too large to drive on normal roads.

A hydraulic piston pushes the cargo bed up to dump the load.

Liquid power

A dumper truck's hopper is powered using telescopic arms. These are arms with a metal piston inside a metal tube. The piston is pushed through the outer tube by liquid such as oil. Using liquid to move objects like this is called hydraulics.

This dumper truck is being filled up with soil by a backhoe loader.

Flatbed trucks

A flatbed truck has a flat trailer bed with no sides or roof. Flatbed trucks are used to carry loads that are very large or have an awkward shape.

Goods can be loaded very easily onto a flatbed trailer. The load slides onto the trailer or the trailer slides underneath the load. The trailers are pulled by powerful tractor units.

TECHNICAL DATA

**Mack Titan
(tractor unit)**

YEARS OF PRODUCTION
2008–present
ENGINE SIZE **16 litres**
NUMBER OF CYLINDERS **6**
TRANSMISSION **Manual**
GEARBOX **10-speed**
NUMBER OF WHEELS **10**
FRONT AXLE WEIGHT
10,400 kg
RADIATOR AREA
11,000 sq cm

Flatbed trailers can be pulled by a wide range of tractor units, such as the heavy-duty Mack Titan, depending on the size of the load.

Sometimes houses have to make way for new roads or railway lines. Brick houses have to be knocked down, but wooden houses can be moved away on a flatbed truck.

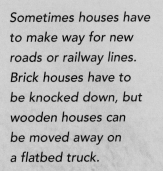

Moving houses

Flatbed trucks can be used to carry whole houses from one place to another. The house is raised up using hydraulic jacks. Wooden beams are then placed under it. The flatbed trailer is positioned underneath the beams, and the house is lowered onto it.

Amazing design

Special extra-strong trailers with lots of wheels are needed to carry the heaviest loads. This factory (right) makes machines for digging tunnels. The huge machines can weigh hundreds of tonnes. Flatbed trucks are used to move heavy parts around the factory. The finished machine is carried out of the factory on a flatbed truck to be loaded onto a train.

Tow trucks

Tow trucks carry other vehicles from one place to another. They are used when vehicles break down or when there is a crash on the roads.

Tow trucks come in many different sizes, depending on the size of the vehicle they need to tow or how badly damaged the vehicle is. The smallest tow trucks are the size of a pickup truck, while the largest are big articulated trucks.

TECHNICAL DATA

Jerr-Dan HPL 6000
YEARS OF PRODUCTION
2005–present
ENGINE SIZE **6.7 litres**
NUMBER OF CYLINDERS **6**
TRANSMISSION **Manual/automatic**
GEARBOX **6-speed**
NUMBER OF WHEELS **6**
LIFTING CAPACITY
FOR WHEEL LIFT
3,000 kg
LIFTING CAPACITY
OF BOOM
6,000 kg

Wheel-lift

Small tow trucks called wheel-lift trucks are modified pickup trucks. The operator fits brackets to the front or rear wheels of the car to be towed. The brackets are fixed in place using steel pins, and the wheels are lifted off the ground. The truck then pulls the car away.

Larger tow trucks carry vehicles on a flatbed. This kind of tow truck is needed when the broken-down vehicle is badly damaged.

A pushback tractor moves a plane around by pulling or pushing on the wheel under the plane's nose.

Amazing design

Special tow trucks called pushback tractors pull and push aeroplanes around airports. Pushback tractors are designed to be very low to the ground so that they fit underneath the plane's nose.

Tow trucks are kept on stand-by at motor races in case of a crash. This Jerr-Dan tow truck lifts the rear of the car using a powerful boom.

Road trains

The largest trucks allowed on the roads are called road trains. These are articulated trucks made up of one tractor unit pulling two or more trailers.

Road trains transport heavy loads in remote parts of the world. They are used in vast countries such as Australia, Canada, Mexico, the United States and Argentina.

Australian giants

The biggest road trains of all are found in Australia, where one tractor unit may pull up to six trailers. Weighing as much as 200 tonnes when full, these are the heaviest vehicles on any road in the world. They carry a wide range of cargo, including livestock, fuel and minerals from mines.

TECHNICAL DATA

ETF Haul Train

YEARS OF PRODUCTION
2010–present

ENGINES **4 engines;**
only 2 engines used when empty

NUMBER OF CYLINDERS
4 per engine

NUMBER OF WHEELS
20 per truck

MAXIMUM LENGTH OF TRAIN
4 trucks

MAXIMUM CARGO WEIGHT
900 tonnes

Road trains are only used in areas where it is very flat. Their engines would not be powerful enough to drive up hills pulling such a huge weight.

An ETF Haul Train uses the combined power of a series of engines to drive up steep hills with heavy loads.

Amazing design

The ETF Haul Train is a special kind of truck designed for use in open-cast mining. The Haul Train is made up of several dumper trucks linked together, each with its own engine. A driver operates the front truck. Signals are sent along wires to all the other trucks to tell them how fast to go and which way to turn. The Haul Train is much more powerful than a road train, which has just one engine at the front.

This huge tractor unit carries a container on its back as well as pulling three trailers behind it. It is transporting minerals from a remote mine in Australia.

Monster trucks

A monster truck is a customised pickup truck, which has had enormous wheels and a very tall suspension added to it.

Monster trucks are built for entertainment, thrilling crowds at shows. They perform tricks or race against each other along obstacle courses.

This monster truck is using its huge wheels to drive over old cars and crush them.

TECHNICAL DATA

Jurassic Attack
YEAR BUILT **1999**
ENGINE SIZE **5.4 litre**
NUMBER OF CYLINDERS **6**
TRANSMISSION **Turbo 400**
HEIGHT **4 m**
WHEEL DIAMETER **1.68 m**
NUMBER OF WHEELS **4**
TYRES **1.7-metre tractor tyres**
WEIGHT **4,500 kg**
FUEL **Alcohol**

This custom-built monster truck is called Jurassic Attack. It has a body shaped like the head of a triceratops dinosaur.

Amazing design

Modern monster trucks are often completely custom-built. They have a specially made tubular chassis, which is light but very strong. The driver sits in the centre of the cab to get the best view. Many of the tricks drivers perform are very dangerous, so the trucks are fitted with lots of safety features. A switch called a 'kill switch' turns off the truck's engine when it crashes to prevent dangerous fires.

Monster Jam

Today there are whole shows dedicated just to monster trucks. The biggest show of all is called Monster Jam. At a Monster Jam show, drivers make spectacular jumps over lines of cars and compete with each other in head-to-head races. The highlight of the show is the freestyle competition, in which the drivers perform tricks such as the wheelie (right).

Glossary

aerodynamic
Shaped to move through the air as easily as possible.

bonnet
The part of a truck's body that opens up to give access to the engine.

brackets
Metal rods placed either side of a car's front wheels so that it can be towed away by a wheel-lift tow truck.

cab
The part of a truck where the driver sits.

chassis
The frame of the truck to which the body and the engine are attached.

customised
Changed from the standard version. Monster trucks are pickup trucks that have been customised by changing the wheels and chassis.

cylinder
A chamber in an engine inside which pistons pump up and down.

exhaust
The waste gases that are made when an engine's fuel is burned. The gases are carried away from the engine along exhaust pipes.

hydraulic jack
A machine powered by liquid that is used to lift heavy objects off the ground.

hopper
An open-topped trailer on the back of a dumper truck used to carry loose material, such as sand or gravel.

gears
A system of cogs that transfers power from the engine to the wheels.

open-cast mine
A mine in which rocks and minerals are taken from the ground by digging a deep pit.

spoiler
A panel attached to the top of the cab to make a truck more aerodynamic.

suspension
A system of springs and shock absorbers that attach the wheels to the chassis. The suspension makes the ride smoother as the truck's wheels pass over bumps. Monster trucks are fitted with very tall suspension to absorb big bumps and jumps.

tractor unit
The front part of an articulated truck, containing the cab and the engine.

trailer
The rear part of an articulated truck. The trailer carries the cargo. It is pulled by a tractor unit.

transmission
The way in which a truck transfers power from the engine to the wheels. The transmission contains a number of different gears.

Models at a glance

Model	Years of Production	Numbers Built	Did You Know?
Peterbilt 389	2006–present	more than 10,000 per year	The 389 has the longest bonnet of any Peterbilt truck. It measures 3.3 m from the front to the back of the cab.
Volvo FM	2008–present	100 dual-fuel models per year	The engine of the dual-fuel FM runs on methane gas and diesel. This makes it very environmentally friendly.
Dodge Ram 1500	2009–present	250,000 per year	The Ram comes in many special versions. The Viper Ram is fast and sporty, with a top speed of 247 kph.
Liebherr T282B	2004–present	up to 50 per year	The T282B is so big that it has to be delivered to mines in parts. The parts are assembled on site.
Mack Titan	2008–present	more than 10,000 per year	The Titan is Mack's largest truck. It is used in logging to carry tree trunks, and also to pull long road trains.
Jerr-Dan HPL 6000	2005–present	more than 1,000 per year	Jerr-Dan make tow trucks by adapting pickup trucks built by companies such as Ford.
ETF Haul Train 152	2010–present	1 truck every 10 days	Haul Trains are fitted with trailers that can dump their load to the back, to the right or to the left.

Websites

www.peterbilt.com

The official website of the Peterbilt truck company, with photos, stats and facts about their latest models.

www.macktrucks.com

The official site of Mack Trucks, with virtual tours inside the cabs of the latest models.

www.etftrucks.eu/Haul-Trains

Animations showing the ETF Haul Train in action.

www.monsterjamonline.co.uk

The website of Monster Jam UK, with photos and videos from past Monster Jam events and information about upcoming events.

www.toptruckgames.com

Lots of free truck games. Race monster trucks, load up a dumper truck or try your hand at parking a long articulated truck.

Index